OCS Study MMS 2005-058

Final Report

Satellite Tracking of Bowhead Whales: The Planning Phase

Lori Quakenbush
Affiliate Assistant Professor
Institute of Marine Science
University of Alaska Fairbanks
loriq@ims.uaf.edu

and

Robert Small
Marine Mammal Program Coordinator
Alaska Department of Fish and Game
Robert_Small@fishgame.state.ak.us

October 2005

Table of Contents

Abstract

Bowhead whales (*Balaena mysticetus*) are managed as an endangered species under the Endangered Species Act due to depletion by commercial whaling during the late 1800s. Bowheads are an important subsistence and cultural resource for coastal people of northern Alaska. Until recently, the entire Bering-Chukchi-Beaufort stock was thought to migrate through the Beaufort Sea twice annually: during their eastward, spring migration and their westward, fall migration. Recent summer sightings indicate some bowheads may stay in the Bering and Chukchi Seas and not enter the Beaufort at all. The importance of the Beaufort Sea for feeding is also in question due to conflicting study results. Oil and gas leasing, exploration, development, and production are ongoing in the Alaskan Beaufort Sea and there is interest in pursuing such activities in the Chukchi Sea. Therefore, greater understanding of bowhead migration and feeding behavior and an increased knowledge of important feeding and summering areas are necessary for the conservation and management of the species. Satellite transmitters deployed on bowhead whales along their migration route can provide information on migration routes, migration timing, swim speed, diving behavior, residence times in portions of their range, and responses to industrial activity. Working with the Alaska Eskimo Whaling Commission (AEWC), the North Slope Borough, the Minerals Management Service, the National Marine Fisheries Service, BP Alaska, Inc., and ConocoPhillips we have cooperatively identified the priority objectives and procedures that are acceptable to all parties. Important components included meeting with and keeping AEWC informed and conducting a workshop that included the assistance of AEWC commissioners to establish priorities and determine feasible methods for attaching transmitters without interfering with subsistence whaling activities.

Introduction

Bowhead whales are the most important species for subsistence communities along the Beaufort Sea coast for both the amount of nutrition and the cultural importance they bring. Subsistence whaling communities are concerned that offshore and nearshore oil and gas activities (e.g., marine seismic projects, offshore oil drilling from ships and islands) may deflect whales away from shore, making hunting more difficult and dangerous, and may displace whales from feeding areas during the short open water season. Oil spills during whale migrations are also of concern.

All bowhead whales from the Bering-Chukchi-Beaufort stock (BCBS), also known as the Western Arctic stock and the Bering stock, are thought to winter in the Bering Sea; however, prior to commercial whaling, some of the population migrated through the Chukchi Sea and into the eastern Canadian Beaufort Sea to summer, while others remained in the Bering Sea (Bockstoce and Botkin 1980). Few bowheads were seen in the Bering or Chukchi Seas during summer shipboard surveys in the 1970s and 1980s (Dahlheim et al. 1980, Miller et al. 1986), leading to speculation that the reduced population now all migrated through the Alaskan Beaufort Sea in spring and fall between wintering and summering areas. In the mid 1980s – early 1990s, however, reports of summer sightings in the western Beaufort Sea near Point Barrow suggested that some bowheads may not be spending summers in the eastern Beaufort Sea (Moore 1992). Sightings in July 1999 near Point Barrow (n = 8) and August 2000 near Cape Simpson (n = 50) indicate that the western Beaufort Sea may be an important summer area (Rugh et al. 2003). Sightings along the Chukotka Peninsula throughout the spring and summer in 1994 (Ainana et al. 1995 and others, summarized in Rugh et al. 2003) may indicate new summer areas are being used as the population continues to increase (George et al. 2004). Based on these combined observations, the presence of a separate stock of bowheads has also been proposed; however, additional research beyond the combined observations from increased survey effort will be required to assess population structure.

The importance of the Beaufort Sea as feeding habitat to bowhead whales has been equivocal. Observations of feeding (Ljungblad et al. 1983, 1986; Lowry and Frost 1984; Moore et al. 1989), prey in stomach contents (Lowry et al. 2004), and isotope ratios of muscle tissue (Hoekstra et al. 2002) have all indicated that substantial feeding occurs in the Beaufort Sea. Two feeding studies (Richardson 1987, Richardson and Thomson 2001) and stable isotope ratios in baleen (Schell et al. 1989, Hobson and Schell 1998, Schell and Saupe 1993) and in baleen and muscle tissue (Lee et al. 2005), however, indicated the amount of energy acquired in the Beaufort was not physiologically significant relative to that acquired in the Bering and Chukchi Seas.

Specifically, isotope ratios in the baleen of adult bowhead whales showed little seasonal change and showed that the major feeding signal came from the Bering and Chukchi Seas in winter (Schell et al. 1989, Hobson and Schell 1998, Schell and Saupe 1993), not from the Beaufort Sea in summer/fall. Subadult whale baleen, however, showed strong seasonal changes between summer (Beaufort) and winter (Bering) with significant feeding in both regions. A more recent study analyzed isotope ratios in bowhead muscle instead of baleen (Hoekstra et al. 2002) and found seasonal fluctuation in carbon isotopes for all age classes, suggesting that the Bering and Beaufort Seas are both important for feeding. Lee et al. (2005), however, got conflicting results in their isotope analysis of muscle tissue from the same whales, and when combined with baleen, their results indicated that the majority of the annual food intake bore the isotope signature of the Bering-Chukchi region, not that of the Beaufort Sea.

Within the Beaufort Sea, the eastern Canadian Beaufort Sea and Amundsen Gulf areas are thought to be used as summer feeding areas for bowhead whales (Fraker and Bockstoce 1980, Würsig et al. 1985), and although feeding has been observed in the Alaskan Beaufort Sea (Ljungblad et al. 1983, 1986; Lowry and Frost 1984; Moore et al. 1989) there is less agreement regarding its relative importance. Richardson (1987) concluded that the bowhead population obtained <1% and <1.4% of its annual energy needs in the Alaskan Beaufort Sea between Kaktovik and Canada in 1985 and 1986, respectively. Another feeding study conducted in 1998–2000 (Richardson and Thomson 2001) concluded that although bowheads in the Alaskan Beaufort Sea spent an average of 47% of their time feeding, they did not obtain more than 5% of their annual energy needs there. Aerial photography and resightings of identifiable individuals was the primary method used to determine residence time for whales in the study area, but this method may have underestimated the amount of time and/or the number of whales feeding there. A significant amount of feeding may also be occurring during behavior that has been recorded as migration (Ljungblad et al. 1986).

Approximately 77% of 137 bowhead whales harvested near Barrow and Kaktovik between 1976 and 2000 had food in their stomachs (Lowry et al. 2004). Subadult bowheads harvested in fall were heavier and had blubber of higher lipid content than those harvested in the spring (Thomson 2002). Stable isotopes, behavioral observations, stomach contents, and lipid levels indicate bowhead whales are feeding in the eastern and western areas of the Beaufort Sea, but further investigation is needed to determine the relative importance of the energy consumed and if the feeding areas are consistent in their location and importance from year to year.

Satellite telemetry is a powerful tool that can be used to address questions regarding marine mammal movements and habitat use (Lowry et al. 2000; Baumgartner and Mate 2001a, b; Dietz et al. 2001; Richard et al. 2001; Boyd et al. 2002). Detailed movements of individual whales can determine residence time in potential feeding areas. Further, satellite transmitters can collect and transmit information on diving behavior in association with location data that can be correlated with feeding and other behaviors. Satellite transmitters were deployed on 12 subadults from the BCBS in the Canadian Beaufort Sea in the fall (Mate et al. 2000). Telemetry data showed that the whales did not move together, and although they spent more time in shallow water, they also used deep water habitats, and they moved through heavy ice and open water (Mate et al. 2000). Satellite telemetry is being successfully used on bowhead whales in Canada and Greenland (Heide-Jørgensen et al. 2003). No tags have been deployed on bowheads of the BCBS in Alaskan waters or during spring or winter.

Our objectives during the planning phase were:

1. Design a study using satellite telemetry as a tool to answer questions regarding bowhead whale migration routes, migration timing, swim speed, diving behavior, residence times in portions of their range, and incidental exposure to industry activity, without interfering with subsistence whaling activities.

2. Provide a forum for collaboration with whaling captains, the Alaska Eskimo Whaling Commission (AEWC), North Slope Borough (NSB), National Marine Fisheries Service, National Oceanic and Atmospheric Administration (NMFS/NOAA), Minerals Management Service (MMS), Alaska Department of Fish and Game (ADF&G) and other interested parties. This forum would provide opportunities for input into the study design and for local involvement in the tagging.

3. Prepare an Implementation Plan to seek three years of funding for satellite tagging and data collection. We will contact other organizations, including the oil and gas industry and NMFS, to explore joint funding possibilities.

Methods

The project objectives were accomplished through communication with all interested parties, presentations at AEWC meetings, and a workshop in Anchorage with representatives from the interested parties.

Results

Objective 1: Study Plan

The Principal Investigators will continue to develop collaborations established during the University of Alaska Coastal Marine Institute Study "Satellite Tracking of Bowhead Whales: The Planning Phase". In order to address all of the objectives, whales will be tagged at multiple locations during the spring and fall migrations. Up to 25 bowhead whales will be tagged in years 2–5. In Year 1 (2005) the number of tags will be limited to 10 due to restrictions of the federal research permit issued by NMFS. An application was submitted in July 2004 to increase the number of transmitters allowed to 25 per year. It is expected that the permit will be modified by 2006.

The objectives of this study include:

Objective 1: Work with the subsistence whalers to deploy satellite transmitters on bowhead whales, of different size categories, in order to document and describe their general pattern of year-round movements.

Objective 2: Use satellite telemetry to document behavior during migration relative to the routes used and the environmental characteristics of those routes; i.e., polynyas, leads, bathymetry, ice conditions, and industrial disturbances.

Objective 3: Document the timing of migration and the rate of travel.

Objective 4: Estimate residence time for individual whales relative to specific geographic locations and/or habitat types.

In Year 1, we will attempt to deploy all 10 tags in the fall at Kaktovik and/or Barrow. If all tags are not deployed in the fall, we will try to deploy the remaining tags from St. Lawrence Island (Gambell or Savoonga) during the winter. Due to open water conditions, St. Lawrence Island whalers have been able to hunt during winter in recent years. In addition to deploying tags, we will also obtain a skin biopsy from each whale receiving a tag. Biopsies will be done by crossbow with a floating biopsy dart. Darts will only penetrate 30 mm. Skin samples will allow us to determine the sex of the bowhead tagged and will be available for genetic analysis.

During tagging the following information will be recorded:

1. Date and time
2. Location (latitude and longitude)
3. Tagger
4. Type of tag
5. Type of boat
6. Number of attempts to tag
7. Distance to target whale when tag deployed
8. Placement of tag on whale, written description and digital photo documentation
9. Reaction of target whale to tag
10. Reaction of target whale to boat
11. Reaction of nearby whales to tagging activity
12. Number of whales in the group
13. Number of calves in the group
14. Approximate length of tagged whale, estimated by whalers
15. Does tagged whale have a calf

In Year 2, we will attempt to deploy 18 tags at St. Lawrence Island (Gambell) in March, prior to the beginning of the spring migration. Tags not deployed there will be made available to be deployed "upstream" along the migration corridor. Point Hope, Wainwright, and Barrow will be locations for spring deployments. Any of these 18 tags not deployed in the spring plus the remaining 7 of the 25 total tags for the year will be deployed in the fall from Kaktovik, Barrow, and possibly Cross Island.

Prior to deployments in Year 3, we will evaluate the data collected to date in order to determine the best allocation of tags by location, season, and bowhead size class.

The principal investigators are dedicated to having Alaska Native subsistence whalers participate in this project in all aspects of planning, development, field logistics, expertise regarding bowhead behavior, and tag deployment whenever possible. We are also dedicated to conducting the tagging without interfering with the bowhead subsistence harvest. If there are acceptable levels of interference those levels will be identified and approved by the whaling captains of the community that would be affected. Without such approval, all tagging will be done without interfering with any whaling activities.

Specific ideas for deploying tags without interfering with whaling are site and season specific. In Barrow during spring, tagging could occur during "cease fires" that are called when the lead is too narrow for whaling. In Barrow and Kaktovik during fall, tagging could occur after the quota was reached for the year by working with a crew dedicated to tagging. Tagging could also occur at Barrow during whaling if the tagging crew worked west of Barrow (downstream of the active whalers). At Gambell and Savoonga if the tags were carried in the whaling boats they could be deployed on whales that were approached but too big for harvest. Near Savoonga in the spring, whales passing by close to the ice edge could by tagged by standing on the ice.

Satellite tags and their attachment technology are improving rapidly. We are communicating with and will likely contract Dr. Mads Peter Heide-Jørgensen, one of the leading experts in telemetry for large cetaceans. Dr. Heide-Jørgensen has configured and deployed over 100 satellite transmitters on bowheads in Canada and Greenland (Heide-Jørgensen et al. 2003, pers. comm.) and his transmitters were used on the northern right whales tagged in the Bering Sea in 2004. Specific tag configuration (type, attachment method, duty cycle, dive data) will be determined soon for the first 10 tags to be deployed in the fall of 2005. We will likely start with a simple tag that records location data only. These tags are less expensive, more reliable, and will last longer. Once we see how the tags deploy and perform we will begin to deploy more sophisticated tags that record dive behavior. There are also tags available that measure oceanographic parameters such as temperature and salinity and we may use these for feeding information. As the project progresses we will continue to evaluate tags and attachments and make adjustments as necessary.

Objective 2: Meetings

Alaska Eskimo Whaling Commission Meeting, 24 June 2004. Lori Quakenbush coordinated with John "Craig" George and Harry Brower Jr. (NSB staff), Charles D. N. Brower (NSB Director), and Maggie Ahmaogak (AEWC Executive Director) for an opportunity to present the satellite tagging study idea at a meeting of the AEWC commissioners in Barrow. Many of the commissioners were present in Barrow, others attended via telephone, and some were absent. The presentation occurred at the end of a long meeting and there were numerous questions. Harry Brower, Jr. suggested that a presentation and discussion be placed on the agenda of the next quarterly AEWC meeting so that all of the commissioners could participate in person in a discussion. The Commissioners agreed that time for a thorough discussion would be best and that having all of the Commissioners present in person would be good. It was agreed to place the satellite telemetry study on the agenda for the quarterly meeting, scheduled to occur on 28 October 2004 in Anchorage.

Alaska Eskimo Whaling Commission Meeting, 28 October 2004. Lori Quakenbush presented the project idea to the AEWC at their quarterly meeting in Anchorage in October 2004 (Appendix A). There was some confusion initially about the details of the tagging study. It was explained that the study details had not yet been determined because we were first seeking approval of the idea from the whalers and then seeking participation by the whalers to determine the study objectives and plan. Once we had their approval we would prepare a study plan with their input. Pursuing a satellite tagging study was approved by the AEWC in a roll call vote, however they wanted to reserve overall support of tagging until they could review and approve a study plan. We also explained that without interest and participation by the whalers we would not pursue the project.

A Work Session for Planning the Study, 18 and 19 January 2005. An agenda and summary are included as Appendix B and C. The work session was held in Anchorage at the Captain Cook. Attendees included:
- Alaska Eskimo Whaling Commission – Harry Brower Jr. (Barrow), George Noongwook (Savoonga), and Merlin Koonooka (Gambell)
- North Slope Borough, Department of Wildlife Management – Charles D. N. Brower and John "Craig" George
- National Marine Fisheries Service – David Rugh
- Minerals Management Service – Chuck Monnett
- ConocoPhillips – Caryn Rea

- BP Alaska – Bill Streever
- Alaska Department of Fish and Game – Robert Small and Lori Quakenbush

The agenda for the Bowhead Tagging Work Session (Appendix B) included background presentations by Lori Quakenbush on the project to date, Craig George on bowhead distribution and stock structure, Chuck Monnett on feeding studies and disturbance, Dave Rugh on migration, and Harry Brower, George Noongwook, and Merlin Koonooka on local knowledge of stocks, feeding, and migration. Lori Quakenbush also described the technology and use of satellite transmitters.

Each participant was invited to state three objectives important to him. Once the objectives were listed, all participants reviewed the objectives to see if any additional ones should be added. We prioritized the objectives by organizing them into similar categories and going through them one by one. Each participant gave a ranking of 1 (high), 2 (moderate), or 3 (low) to each objective. The priorities, their sponsors, and their rankings are included in Appendix C.

Priority objectives identified by the workshop participants included:
- Determine the summer distribution of bowhead whales in the Bering, Chukchi, and Beaufort Seas
- Identify places where bowhead whales aggregate; i.e., wintering, feeding, breeding areas
- Document annual variability in the migration route
- Determine if there are long-term effects of industrial activity to bowhead whales
- Document early spring movements of bowhead whales near St. Lawrence Island to define the beginning of the migration

There was a keen interest in the stock structure question posed by IWC. Whether the BCBS of bowheads is made up of two stocks is in question. If there were two stocks then IWC would want to manage them as two and have separate harvest quotas for each. Funding is available through NMFS/NOAA to address this question and a study plan has been developed (Moore and George 2005). AEWC commissioners are mixed in their opinions about seeking information to determine if multiple stocks exist. Much of the information collected by satellite telemetry to address our priority objectives may also be useful to address stock structure.

We also discussed how to approach whales for tagging without interfering with subsistence whaling. At Barrow in spring, tagging could occur during "cease fires," called when hunting conditions are poor and the risk of a strike without landing a whale are too high. Tagging could occur either with the help of a crew or by standing on the lead edge. In Barrow and Kaktovik during fall, tagging could occur after the quota was reached for the year by working with a crew dedicated to tagging. Tagging could also occur at Barrow during whaling if the tagging crew worked west of Barrow (downstream of the active whalers). At Gambell and Savoonga, if the tags were carried in the whaling boats they could be deployed on whales that were approached but too big for harvest. Near Savoonga in the spring, whales passing by close to the ice edge could by tagged by someone standing on the ice.

Alaska Eskimo Whaling Commission Meeting, 3 February 2005. Lori Quakenbush presented an update of the tagging project and the results of the January work session to AEWC at their Mini Convention in Barrow. Questions and concerns raised at this meeting included the impact of the tags on the whales, interference with subsistence whaling, and whether the IWC would consider deploying tags as strikes.

It was important to the whalers that the tags be designed to have minimal long-term impacts on the whale's health. It was pointed out that two of eight whales that were tagged with VHF radio transmitters in the eastern Beaufort in Canadian waters (Wartzok et al. 1990) were harvested at Gambell.

It was stressed that it would not be acceptable for the study to interfere with whaling activities. There were also questions about the IWC's definition of a strike and whether tags would count against the strike quota. Although it was explained that the tagging would be done under a NMFS research permit that would be independent of the quota even if whalers were deploying the tags, there is still some concern and skepticism that we need to address. More concern over stock structure led to how the results from tagging may be used to show separate stocks exist and how that would not be good for the whalers. Whereas it is true that telemetry data may be used to argue for the two-stock theory, it may also give evidence supporting one stock. We were reminded that the strength and tradition of AEWC and NSB, especially where IWC is concerned, has been their willingness to collect and present information regardless of its content. A resolution was passed to withdraw support if evidence of harm to the whales was discovered or if any interference with subsistence whaling activities occurred.

Bowhead Genetic Workshop, Seattle, Washington, 23 and 24 February 2005. A workshop titled "Workshop on Bowhead Whale Stock Structure Studies in the Bering-Chukchi-Beaufort Seas: 2005–2006" was sponsored by the Alaska Fisheries Science Center and National Marine Mammal Laboratory of NOAA and NSB to address IWC's multiple stock concerns. Lori Quakenbush was invited to present a summary of the satellite-tagging project. Satellite tagging designed to learn about migration, feeding, and areas of concentration were of great interest because this type of information would also help to determine the stock structure. At this workshop NOAA, NSB, and others were preparing a plan to study stock structure within the BCBS. Satellite-tagging was also a component of their stock structure study plan, yet funding does not allow them to begin tagging before 2007.

Objective 3: Implementation Plan

Minerals Management Service is funding a study to be managed by the Alaska Department of Fish and Game (ADF&G) working in close cooperation with Alaska Native subsistence whalers, in which the whalers will participate in the study by providing logistics, bowhead behavior expertise, and by deploying the tags whenever possible. Satellite telemetry will be used to document year-round movements of bowhead whales throughout their range. The satellite telemetry study is one of four contracts supported under a multidisciplinary study entitled "Bowhead Whale Feeding in the Central and Western Alaskan Beaufort Sea". Other contracts will support research on: 1) bowhead whale feeding behavior and prey distributions; 2) oceanographic conditions associated with feeding bowheads and their prey; and 3) integration and synthesis of the research. This is a 5-year study in which ADF&G will provide technical and analytical expertise, administrative support, and oversight in the study and subsistence whalers will provide expertise in aspects of field logistics and bowhead whale behavior resulting in the whaler's deployment of the satellite tags whenever possible.

We expect that the Request for Proposal from MMS to ADF&G will be received in early July 2005 and that 10 tags will be deployed in September and October 2005.

Discussion

Learning more about bowhead whales was the goal of all the interested parties. We determined initially that interference with the subsistence harvest was not acceptable for this study. When and where to deploy tags was driven by the need to avoid interfering with the subsistence harvest. AEWC commissioners determined where, when, and how tags could be put on that would not affect whaling. Using that information, combined with the need for information on bowhead movements throughout the year, lead to a study design that was acceptable to all.

We have successfully accomplished our objectives and are ready to move into the study phase. The study plan will be presented to AEWC for their approval during the summer of 2005 and we will continue to work with whalers from each village as the project develops. The contract with MMS is being developed, the funding is available, and this cooperative project is moving forward with all interested parties participating.

Acknowledgments

John "Craig" George and Todd O'Hara were instrumental in initiating the project. Charles D. N. Brower, Harry Brower, Jr., and Robert Suydam, all of the NSB, provided key ideas during the early planning stages. Maggie Ahmaogak and Thomas Napagiak, Jr. of the AEWC were gracious in including our presentations on their already full agenda. George Noongwook, Merlin Koonooka, and Harry Brower Jr. of the AEWC provided extremely useful ideas and information during the January work session to help determine the objectives of the study and how to achieve them. Chuck Monnett, MMS; Dave Rugh, NMFS; Caryn Rea, ConocoPhillips; and Bill Strever, BP Alaska, Inc., also contributed greatly to the work session. This study was funded in part by Cooperative Agreement No. 0102CA85294, Task Order 35248, between the University of Alaska and the Minerals Management Service. We thank the NSB for matching funds and facilitation.

Study Products

1) Summaries of the meetings and workshop are included in this report as appendices.
2) A study design for using satellite telemetry to provide information on year-round bowhead whale behavior, while not interfering with subsistence whaling, is included in the body of this final report.
3) The application for a scientific research permit to place up to 25 transmitters per year on bowhead whales in the U.S. has been submitted to NOAA, NMFS, Office of Protected Resources by NMFS, National Marine Mammal Laboratory and is under review. We will be allowed to tag up to 10 bowhead whales in 2005 under Scientific Research Permit No. 782-1719.
4) Funding has been secured through MMS for a five-year study to tag 10 bowhead whales in 2005 and up to 25 in 2006–2010.
5) Annual Report. Quakenbush, L.T. and R.J. Small. 2005. Satellite tracking of bowhead whales: The planning process, p. 132–136. *In* University of Alaska Coastal Marine Institute Annual Report No. 11. OCS Study MMS 2005-xxx, University of Alaska Fairbanks and USDOI, MMS, Alaska OCS Region.

References

Ainana, L., N. Mymrin, L. Bogoslavskaya, and I. Zagrebin. 1995. Role of the Eskimo Society of Chukotka in encouraging traditional native use of wildlife resources by Chukotka Natives and in conducting shore-based observations on the distribution of bowhead whales, *Balaena mysticetus*, in coastal waters off the south-eastern part of the Chukotka Peninsula (Russia) during 1994. Report by the Eskimo Society of Chukotka to the Department of Wildlife Management, North Slope Borough, Barrow, Alaska. 135 pp.

Baumgartner, M. F., and B. R. Mate. 2001a. Understanding the relationship between North Atlantic right whale movements and habitat characteristics from satellite-monitored radio tag data: A novel approach. 14th Biennial Conference on the Biology of Marine Mammals. Vancouver, Canada, November 28 – December 3, 2001 (Abstract).

Baumgartner, M. F., and B. R. Mate. 2001b. Summer feeding season movements and fall migration of North Atlantic right whales from satellite-monitored radio tags. 14th Biennial Conference on the Biology of Marine Mammals. Vancouver, Canada, November 28 – December 3, 2001 (Abstract).

Bockstoce, J. R., and D. B. Botkin. 1980. The historical status and reduction of the western Arctic bowhead whale (*Balaena mysticetus*) population by the pelagic whaling industry, 1848–1914. New Bedford Whaling Museum, New Bedford MA. 160 pp. Final report to the National Marine Fisheries Service by the Old Dartford Historical Society 03-78-MO2-2012.

Boyd, I. L., I. J. Staniland, and A. R. Martin. 2002. Distribution of foraging by female Antarctic fur seals. Marine Ecology Progress Series 242: 285–294.

Dahleim, M., T. Bray, and H. Braham. 1980. Vessel survey for bowhead whales in the Bering and Chukchi Seas, June–July, 1978. Marine Fisheries Review. 42(9–10):51–57.

Dietz, R., M. P. Heide-Jørgensen, P. R. Richard, and M. Acquarone. 2001. Summer and fall movements of narwhals (*Monodon monoceros*) from Northeastern Baffin Island towards Northern Davis Strait. Arctic 54(3):244–261.

Fraker, M. A., and J. R. Bockstoce. 1980. Summer distribution of bowhead whales in the eastern Beaufort Sea. Marine Fisheries Review 42(9–10):57–64.

George, J. C., J. Zeh, R. Suydam, and C. Clark. 2004. Abundance and population trend (1978–2001) of western Arctic bowhead whales surveyed near Barrow, Alaska. Marine Mammal Science 20(4):755–773.

Heide-Jørgensen, M. P., K. L. Laidre, Ø. Wiig, M. V. Jensen, L. Dueck, L.D. Maiers, H. C. Schmidt, and R. C. Hobbs. 2003. From Greenland to Canada in ten days: tracks of bowhead whales, *Balaena mysticetus*, across Baffin Bay. Arctic 56(1):21–31.

Hoekstra, P. F., L. A. Dehn, J. C. George, K. R. Solomon, D. C. G. Muir, and T. M. O'Hara. 2002. Trophic ecology of bowhead whales (*Balaena mysticetus*) compared with that of other arctic marine biota as interpreted from carbon-, nitrogen-, and sulfur-isotope signatures. Canadian Journal of Zoology, 80:223–231.

Hobson, K. A., and D. M. Schell. 1998. Stable carbon and nitrogen isotope patterns in baleen from eastern Arctic bowhead whales (*Balaena mysticetus*). Canadian Journal of Fisheries and Aquatic Sciences 55:2601–2607.

Lee, S. H., D. M. Schell, T. L. McDonald, and W. J. Richardson. 2005. Regional and seasonal feeding by bowhead whales (*Balaena mysticetus*) as indicated by stable isotope ratios. Marine Ecology Progress Series 285:271–287.

Ljungblad, D. K., S. E., Moore, and D. R. Van Schoik. 1983. Aerial surveys of endangered whales in the Beaufort, eastern Chukchi and northern Bering Seas, 1982. NOSC Technical Document 605. Report from Naval Ocean Systems Center, Dan Diego, CA for U.S. Minerals Management Service, Anchorage, AK. 382 pp. (NTIS AD-A134 772/3).

Ljungblad, D. K., S. E., Moore, and J. T. Clarke. 1986. Assessment of bowhead whale (*Balaena mysticetus*) feeding patterns in the Alaskan Beaufort and northeastern Chukchi Seas via aerial surveys, fall 1979–1984. Report of the International Whaling Commission 336:265–272.

Lowry, L. F., and K. J. Frost. 1984. Foods and feeding of bowhead whales in western and northern Alaska. Scientific Reports of the Whales Research Institute, Tokyo 35:1–16.

Lowry, L. F., G. Sheffield, and J. C. George. 2004. Bowhead whale feeding in the Alaskan Beaufort Sea, based on stomach contents analysis. Journal of Cetacean Research Management 6(3):215–223.

Lowry, L. F., V. N. Burkanov, K. J. Frost, M. A. Simpkins, R. Davis, D. P. Demaster, R. Suydam, and A. Springer. 2000. Habitat use and habitat selection by spotted seals (*Phoca largha*) in the Bering Sea. Canadian Journal of Zoology 78:1959–1971.

Mate, B. R., G. K, Krutzikowsky, and M. H. Winsor. 2000. Satellite-monitored movements of radio-tagged bowhead whales in the Beaufort and Chukchi Seas during the late-summer feeding season and fall migration. Canadian Journal of Zoology. 78(7):1168–1181.

Miller, R. V., D. J. Rugh, and J. H. Johnson. 1986. The distribution of bowhead whales, *Balaena mysticetus*, in the Chukchi Sea. Marine Mammal Science. 2:214–222.

Moore, S. E. 1992. Summer records of bowhead whales in the northeastern Chukchi Sea. Arctic 45(4):398–400.

Moore, S. E., J. T. Clarke, and D. K. Ljungblad. 1989. Bowhead whale (*Balaena mysticetus*) spatial and temporal distribution in the central Beaufort Sea during late summer and early fall 1979–86. Report to the International Whaling Commission 39:283–290.

Moore, S. E., and J. C. George. Convenors. 2005. Workshop on bowhead whale stock structure studies in the Bering-Chukchi-Beaufort Seas: 2005–2006.

Richard, P. R., M. P. Heide-Jørgensen, J. R. Orr, R. Dietz, and T. G. Smith. 2001. Summer and autumn movements and habitat use by belugas in the Canadian High Arctic and adjacent areas. Arctic 54 (3): 207–222.

Richardson, W. J., ed. 1987. Importance of the eastern Alaskan Beaufort Sea to feeding bowhead whales, 1985–1986. Report by LGL Ecological Research Associates Inc. to U.S. Minerals Management Service. NTIS No. PB 88 150271/AS. 131 pp.

Richardson, W. J., and D. H. Thomson, eds. 2001. Bowhead whale feeding in the eastern Alaskan Beaufort Sea: update of scientific and traditional information. Draft Final Report by LGL Limited, Environmental Research Associates and LGL Ecological Research Associates Inc. to U.S. Minerals Management Service MMS# 1435-01-97-/CT-30842. 2 Vols.

Rugh, D., D. Demaster, A. Rooney, J. Breiwick, K. Shelden, and S. Moore. 2003. A review of bowhead whale (*Balaena mysticetus*) stock identity. Journal of Cetacean Research and Management 5(3):267–279.

Schell, D. M., S. M. Saupe, and N. Haubenstock. 1989. Bowhead whale (*Balaena mysticetus*) growth and feeding as estimated by $\delta^{13}C$ techniques. Marine Biology (Berl.) 103:433–443.

Schell, D. M., and S. M. Saupe. 1993. Feeding and growth as indicated by stable isotopes. Pages 491–509 *in* The bowhead whale. J. J. Burns, J. J. Montague, and C. J. Cowles, eds. Special Publication No. 2, The Society for Marine Mammalogy, Lawrence, KS.

Thomson, D. H. 2002. Energetics of bowhead whales. *In:* W. J. Richardson and D. H. Thomson (eds.), Bowhead Whale Feeding in the Eastern Alaskan Beaufort Sea: Update of Scientific and Traditional Information, Vol. 2, Chapter 22. OCS Study MMS 2002-012. LGL Report TA2196-7. Report from LGL Ltd., King City, Ontario Canada to U.S. Minerals Management Service Anchorage, AK.

Wartzok, D., W. A. Watkins, B. Würsig, J. Guerrero, and J. Schoenherr. 1990. Movements and behavior of bowhead whales. Report from Purdue University, Fort Wayne, Indiana for Amoco Production Co., P.O. Box 800, Denver, CO 80201, USA.

Würsig, B., E. M. Dorsey, M. A. Fraker, R. S. Payne, and W. J. Richardson. 1985. Behavior of bowhead whales, *Balaena mysticetus*, summering in the Beaufort Sea: a description. Fishery Bulletin 83:357–377.

Handout for the Alaska Eskimo Whaling Commission Meeting, 28 October 2004.

Bowhead Tagging – the planning phase

Background: Bowhead whales are the most important species for subsistence communities along the Chukchi and Beaufort sea coasts. Concerns regarding bowheads include:

Offshore and nearshore oil and gas activities

- may deflect whales away from shore making hunting more difficult and dangerous
- may displace whales from feeding areas
- may cause oil spills that would affect migrating bowheads

Stock structure

- IWC is concerned that whales harvested at St. Lawrence Island may be a different stock than those harvested at Barrow

General behavior

- migration routes
- migration timing
- feeding areas
- diving behavior
- time spent in areas within spring and summer range

These issues can all be addressed using satellite telemetry as a tool to determine bowhead movements and diving/surfacing behavior.

1st Step: The Minerals Management Service, the Alaska Dept. of Fish and Game, and the North Slope Borough were interested in what could be learned by tagging bowheads and put together money and other support to discuss the idea with the AEWC Commissioners. The idea was presented to Maggie Ahmaogak in May 2004 and she invited me to speak to the AEWC Commissioners at your meeting in Barrow in June 2004. After an introduction and short discussion it was determined that a longer discussion with more Commissioners present would be best and bowhead tagging was put on the agenda for this meeting (October 2004).

2nd Step: Without your approval this project will not happen. If the study is approved it must be conducted without interfering with subsistence whaling activities. With your approval this project could proceed in at least 2 ways:

1) AEWC Commissioners could be involved in designing and conducting the study. That could include:
   a) Determine the most important questions to answer
   b) Determine which transmitters to use
   c) Determine when, where, and how to put transmitters on
   d) Put the transmitters on

2) AEWC Commissioners could approve the study but not be involved directly in designing and conducting the study.

3rd Step: If this study is approved by AEWC Commissioners the next step is to have a workshop with AEWC representatives, North Slope Borough, Mineral Management Service, National Marine Fisheries Service, Alaska Dept. of Fish and Game, and oil company representatives to design the study. It was suggested that having a workshop in conjunction with the AEWC mini-convention in February 2005 would be a good time for AEWC Commissioners to participate.

If this study is not approved by AEWC Commissioners then I would drop my efforts to organize it. I think this project has the greatest potential for learning the most about bowheads if AEWC and the whalers are involved.

4th Step: Only if approved. Secure the funding and start tagging.

Submitted to AEWC 28 October 2004 by:

Lori Quakenbush
Wildlife Biologist
Arctic Marine Mammals
Alaska Department of Fish and Game
1300 College Road
Fairbanks, AK 99701
Ph: (907) 459-7214; Fax: (907) 452-6410
Lori_quakenbush@fishgame.state.ak.us

Appendix B. Agenda for Tagging Work Session, 18 and 19 January 2005.

Satellite Tracking of Bowhead Whales: The Planning Phase
A Work Session for Planning the Study

AGENDA
Tuesday, 18 January 2005
9:00 am – 4:30 pm
Captain Cook, Club Room, Anchorage

8:45   Coffee

9:00   **Introductions**

Purpose of the Workshop

Background Presentations

Project to Date	Lori Quakenbush (ADF&G)
Distribution	Craig George (NSB)
Genetics/Stock Structure	Craig George
Feeding Studies and Disturbance	Chuck Monnett (MMS)
Migration	Dave Rugh (NMFS), Chuck Monnett, Craig George
Local Knowledge of Stocks, Feeding, Migration	Harry Brower, George Noongwook, Merlin Koonooka (AEWC)
Satellite Transmitters	Lori Quakenbush

Reiteration of Purpose of Workshop

12:00-1:30 **Lunch**

Identify Objectives

Each participant state 3 objectives important to them
(Objectives do not have to be different from those already stated)

Review Objectives

Are any objectives missing that should be included?

Prioritize Objectives

4:30 **Recess**

17

Satellite Tracking of Bowhead Whales: The Planning Phase
A Work Session for Planning the Study

AGENDA
Wednesday, 19 January 2005
9:00 am – 1:00 pm
Captain Cook, Club Room, Anchorage

9:00   Coffee

9:15   **Review Prioritized Objectives**

       Design Study to Meet Objectives

             Location of tagging

             Time of year for tagging

             Sample size

             Data to be collected by tag (e.g. location, dive, oceanographic)

1:00   **Adjourn**

Appendix C. Summary of Bowhead Satellite Tracking Work Session, 18 and 19 January 2005

The purpose of this workshop is to:
1. Identify and prioritize objectives regarding bowhead whales that can be addressed using satellite telemetry for incorporation into a study design.

   Such objectives could include:
   - Migration routes
   - Migration timing
   - Influence of ice
   - Water depth
   - Movement patterns
   - Swim speed
   - Feeding behavior
   - Diving behavior
   - Residence times in various regions
   - Behavior near industrial activity
   - Stock assessment

2. Design a study using satellite telemetry as a tool to address priority objectives.
   The study must be designed so as not to interfere with subsistence whaling and it is preferred that tags will be put on by whalers, if at all possible.

Attendees included:
- Alaska Eskimo Whaling Commission – Harry Brower Jr. (Barrow), George Noongwook (Savoonga), and Merlin Koonooka (Gambell)
- North Slope Borough, Department of Wildlife Management – Charles D. N. Brower, and John "Craig" George
- National Marine Fisheries Service – David Rugh
- Minerals Management Service – Chuck Monnett
- ConocoPhillips – Caryn Rea
- BP Alaska – Bill Streever
- Alaska Department of Fish and Game – Robert Small, and Lori Quakenbush

Background Presentations included:

Project to Date – Lori Quakenbush gave an overview of the project to date. Tagging bowheads in Alaskan waters has been talked about for many years; however, issues with the status of the population and the IWC quota have kept it from being considered seriously. Currently, with acceptance of a population estimate of 8,100–13,500 (Craig et al. 2004) and a quota that meets current needs, remaining questions about migration, important habitats, and effects of industry have renewed interest in using satellite telemetry as a tool to learn more about bowhead whales.

The first objective of the project is to design a study using satellite transmitters as a tool to answer questions regarding bowhead whale migration, feeding areas, wintering areas, and behavior around industrial activity, **without interfering with subsistence whaling**. Stock structure was not originally considered an objective of this study, but could be if desired. The second objective is to provide a forum for collaboration with whaling captains, AEWC, NSB, NMFS, MMS, oil industry, and other interested parties. This forum would provide opportunities for input into the study design and for whalers to be involved in the tagging.

Meetings attended where the tagging project was presented include:

6 May 2004 – Met with Maggie Ahmaogak, received invitation to AEWC meeting on 24 June 2004.

24 June 2004 – Presented project to AEWC at a special meeting in Barrow. Topic was deferred to a Quarterly meeting in Anchorage for more time and more commissioners present for discussion.

28 October 2004 – Project presented to AEWC at Quarterly meeting in Anchorage. Approval to pursue a satellite tagging study as described was granted by a unanimous roll call vote. AEWC agreed to support the planning of the project but would reserve overall support of tagging until they could review and approve a study plan.

Bowhead Genetics/Stock Structure – Craig George summarized a recent concern of IWC on the stock structure of the Bering-Chukchi-Beaufort (BCB) stock of bowheads.

Bowhead Feeding Studies – Chuck Monnett summarized feeding studies in the Beaufort Sea. MMS recognizes that bowheads are feeding in the Beaufort Sea but they are trying to understand it better by addressing questions such as: 1) How much feeding occurs in the Beaufort Sea, and 2) How predictable is the time and place where feeding occurs? Answers to these questions are necessary in order to manage oil activity near the feeding areas.

Bowhead Disturbance Studies – Chuck Monnett summarized several disturbance studies sponsored by MMS.

Local Knowledge of Stocks, Feeding, Migration – Merlin Koonooka from Gambell, George Noongwook from Savoonga, and Harry Brower, Jr. from Barrow shared their knowledge of bowhead whale feeding, migration, and possible stock structure from their different regional perspectives.

Satellite Transmitters – Lori Quakenbush gave a summary of what satellite transmitters are, how they work, what they do, and what is currently available. Information that can be collected includes: 1) location only, 2) location and depth information from diving, and 3) location and oceanographic information (i.e., water temperature and/or salinity).

Note: Bowhead Distribution and Bowhead Migration were on the agenda as Background Presentations but were not presented as individual topics.

Identification of Study Objectives. Each participant was invited to offer three objectives.

Merlin Koonooka
1) What are long-term affects of industrial activity? Could industrial noise cause stranding events like those that occur with other whales?
2) What are the effects of a warming climate on bowheads? Warming could change the migration routes past St. Lawrence Island.
3) Show that bowheads are only one stock.

Harry Brower
Document migration routes and migration timing. Ice is changing. Diomede, Kivalina, and Wales are no longer able to get out on the ice to hunt now. Bowheads are arriving earlier in the spring, but there is less daylight. Bowheads also are traveling along offshore leads more and less on nearshore leads.

Craig George
1) Document movements of whales along Chukotka coast in summer. St. Lawrence whalers say some whales don't go by Barrow and some counts along the Russian coast
2) Document movements of whales near St. Lawrence Island in spring and compare to Traditional Ecological Knowledge.
3) Document bowhead response to disturbance by tagging near Kaktovik and tracking whales as they move through the oilfield.

Dave Rugh
Document summer distribution in Bering and Chukchi Seas and near Barrow.

George Noongwook
1) Document migration routes and timing
2) Document spring migration near St. Lawrence Island. When does migration start? It may start earlier than when whalers begin whaling in April. Whalers may miss the small whales by starting to hunt in April.
3) Document residence times in various regions. Where are the winter areas? Is there segregation by size in different winter areas? Harry says small whales get to Barrow first, maybe they winter together somewhere.

Chuck Monnett
1) Test current theory about migration route and identify deviations vs. constancy among years
2) Identify places whales aggregate and determine if there are any demographic patterns
3) Determine residence times for aggregations

Caryn Rea
Her general desire is to have location specific data available about bowheads so that when oil exploration is planned in a specified area drilling could be done with appropriate mitigation to protect bowheads.
1) Determine effects of disturbance
2) Document migration routes and movements
3) Identify areas where whales spend time

Prioritized Study Objectives. Study objectives were consolidated and rated by each participant for importance (1 = high, 2 = moderate, 3 = low). An overall rank was established (1–7) with 1 being most important.

Over all Rank	Name	Objectives	Rank [1=high]
7	HB	Opportunistic tagging to study effects of ice-breaker noise on whale behavior and migratory paths. [Comments: ice breakers form leads and whales sometimes follow them, TEK suggests whales were diverted ~ 30 miles offshore near Pt. Hope; disturbance is also an issue]	2,2,3,2,3,3 (15)
2	CM; CR	Test current theory about migration routes; identify deviations and consistency between years. [Comments: high variability; problem of tagging different whales between years.]	1,1,1,2,1,1 (7)
3	CM	Identify places whales aggregate and determine if there are demographic patterns (i.e., mother-calf pairs, size, age, migration timing) and where they occur. [Comments: could note changes in distributions]	1,2,1,2,1,2 (9)
4	CM; CR	Residence times: how long do whales remain in aggregation areas (on a scale of days). [Comments: general applications not just to feeding-days]	1,2,2,2,2,1 (10)
2	MK	Behavior, short and long-term effects of industrial activity/exposure (Comments: difficult to determine cause and effect; what if activity has a long-term effect?, how do you study long-term chronic effects? question of how effective tagging will be in answering this; already several studies underway looking at this (BP, BWASP)	1,1,1,2,1,1 (7)
5	HB; GN; MK	Effects of climate warming on: a) whale health, b) changing migration paths and timing due to ice conditions, c) later return of whales to SLI in fall. [Comments: hunting period is limited by daylight and temperature while migration is getting earlier (at Barrow), whales traveling more on 'far side' of the lead; can make better hunting decisions with this information; tagging might help us understand these relationships, e.g., sea ice vs. whales; so far animals appear healthy but see projections where changes to prey base is predicted]	1,2,1,2,2,3 (11)
1	CG; DR; MK	Stock Differentiation: **A)** Summer distribution in the Bering and Chukchi and Barrow area via tagging in late spring or summer (during feeding season); [Comments: includes movements of whales along the Chukotka coast in summer, follow whales into wintering areas; Barrow hunters do not have "problems" with current situation, science/political drivers]. **B)** Use tagging to determine if there is more than one stock at SLI; Noted on increasing numbers of whales at SLI; is this a different stock or a growing large stocks?	1,1,1,1,1,1 (6)
2	CG; DR; GN	Spring movements of whales near SLI to define migratory routes [comments: focus during breeding season and demographics of whales (large vs. small, size, sex) in spring near SLI]	1,1,2,1,1,1 (7)
6	CG; DR; CR	Disturbance: Within-year industrial disturbance study via tagging at the Canadian border with special focus on the mid-Beaufort area; include passive-acoustic buoys to monitor ambient noise; control area might be east of Kaktovik. (Comments: BWASP surveys are designed to look at whale distribution through time; in pre-industrial period whales were closer to shore; surveys started after disturbance had occurred so may not detect effect)	1,2,2,2,2,3 (12)
1	GN; (BT)	Specific question about where bowheads are wintering. Is there spatial segregation during winter? [Comments: sex, age stocking, the winter question might be achieved by tagging near Barrow in fall and following whales into wintering areas]	1,1,1,1,1,1 (6)

HB = Harry Brower, Jr.; CM = Chuck Monnett; CR = Caryn Rea; MK = Merlin Koonooka; GN = George Noongwook; DR = Dave Rugh

Other Discussions.

We also discussed how to deploy tags on whales without interfering with subsistence whaling. In Barrow, spring tagging could occur during "cease fires" called when hunting conditions are poor and the risk of a strike without landing a whale are too high. Tagging could occur either with the help of a crew or by standing on the lead edge. In Barrow and Kaktovik, during fall, tagging could occur after the quota was reached for the year by working with a crew dedicated to tagging. Tagging could also occur at Barrow during whaling if the tagging crew worked west of Barrow (downstream of the active whalers). At Gambell and Savoonga if the tags were carried in the whaling boats they could be deployed on whales that were approached but too big for harvest. Near Savoonga in the spring, whales passing by close to the ice edge could be tagged by standing on the ice.

Design Study to Meet Objectives.

We ran out of time to address this agenda item, however, the discussion and prioritization of objectives provided the information needed to design the study to meet the objectives.

Literature Cited.

George, J. C., J. Zeh, R. Suydam, and C. Clark. 2004. Abundance and population trend (1978–2001) of western Arctic bowhead whales surveyed near Barrow, Alaska. Marine Mammal Science 20(4): 755–773.

Appendix D. Bowhead Whale Satellite Tagging Project Update to AEWC, 3 February 2005.

Bowhead Whale Satellite Tagging Project – Planning Phase Update

Objective 1: Design a study using satellite transmitters as a tool to answer questions regarding bowhead whale migration, feeding areas, wintering areas, and behavior around industrial activity, **without interfering with subsistence whaling.** Stock structure was not an original objective of this study but could be, if desired.

Objective 2: Provide a forum for collaboration with whaling captains, AEWC, NSB, NMFS, MMS, oil industry, and other interested parties. This forum would provide opportunities for input into the study design and for whalers to be involved in the tagging.

HISTORY

6 May 2004: Met with Maggie Ahmaogak, received invitation to AEWC meeting

24 June 2004: Presented Project to AEWC at a special meeting in Barrow.

28 October 2004: Presented Project to AEWC at Quarterly meeting in Anchorage. Pursuing a satellite tagging study was approved by a role call vote. AEWC agreed to support the planning of the project but would reserve overall support of tagging until they could review and approve a study plan.

18 – 19 January 2005: Workshop to identify and prioritize objectives regarding bowhead whales that can be addressed using satellite telemetry. Begin to design a study. **Study must not interfere with subsistence whaling** and it is preferred that tags be put on by whalers, if possible.

Workshop was attended by AEWC representatives (Harry Brower, Jr., George Noongwook, Merlin Koonooka), NSB (Craig George, Charles Brower), NMFS (Dave Rugh), MMS (Chuck Monnett), Oil Industry (Caryn Rea, Bill Streever), ADF&G (Lori Quakenbush, Bob Small).

Priority objectives identified by the workshop participants included:
- Summer distribution in the Bering, Chukchi, and Beaufort Seas
- Identify places where whales aggregate (wintering and feeding areas)
- Document variability in migration route from year to year
- Determine if there are long-term effects of industrial activity to bowheads
- Document early spring movements of whales near St Lawrence Island to define the beginning of the migration

3 February 2005: Presented an update of the tagging project to AEWC at the Mini Convention in Barrow.

Next Step: Develop study plan and present to AEWC.

Submitted to AEWC 3 February 2005 by:

Lori Quakenbush, Wildlife Biologist
Arctic Marine Mammals, Alaska Department of Fish and Game
1300 College Road, Fairbanks, AK 99701
Ph: (907) 459-7214; Fax: (907) 452-6410
Lori_quakenbush@fishgame.state.ak.us